50 Things Every Catholic Should Know

PREPARING FOR CONFIRMATION

50 Things Every Catholic Should Know

PREPARING FOR CONFIRMATION

Archdiocese of Kansas City in Kansas

Preface by Archbishop Joseph F. Naumann

EMMAUS ROAD PUBLISHING

Steubenville, Ohio
A Division of Catholics United for the Faith
www.emmausroad.org

Emmaus Road Publishing
827 North Fourth Street
Steubenville, Ohio 43952

Library of Congress Control Number: 2014954190
ISBN: 978-1-63446-005-7

Layout and Design by:
Theresa Westling

Cover image:
The Eternal Father (oil on canvas), Veronese, (Paolo Caliari) (1528-88)/
Hospital Tavera, Toledo, Spain / Bridgeman Images

March 19, 2014
St. Joseph, Spouse of the BVM

One of my greatest joys as an Archbishop is to celebrate the Sacrament of Confirmation with young men and women from parishes across northeast Kansas. I rely heavily on the teachers, formation teams, and above all the parents to ensure that these young people approach the sacrament prepared to embrace more fully the reality of Jesus Christ and the truth, beauty, and goodness He has revealed.

While knowing and loving the Lord is most important, knowing the content and meaning of what He has revealed and the implications of that revelation in the Christian life are also necessities in the sacramental preparation process. To that end, I have developed a list of fifty (50) questions that I think every young person preparing for Confirmation should be able to answer. This booklet contains those questions and provides the sources where the answers to the questions can be found. I not only encourage the use this booklet for those preparing for Confirmation, but really for all those who want to know the basic teachings of the Catholic Church.

These are not necessarily the most important questions related to the faith, and by no means does this booklet attempt to provide a comprehensive exploration of the entire content of the faith. In fact, the questions are somewhat arbitrary. They do not, for example, address the Church's extensive social teaching, which is especially important for older teens and young adults as they prepare to apply timeless Christian principles in today's challenging, rapidly changing world. Nevertheless, I firmly believe that every adult Catholic should be able to answer the questions in this booklet.

In short, this booklet is intended to support and supplement the vital work of religious education and sacramental preparation that is going on in families, parishes, schools, and small faith-sharing groups throughout the world, offering straightforward responses to many of the most basic questions regarding our Catholic faith.

I want to take this opportunity to thank in a particular way all those who put forth the time, effort, and devotion to prepare our young people for the Sacrament of Confirmation. It is a most significant step in their ongoing journey as disciples of the Lord Jesus. May He strengthen you and sustain you in all your efforts. May the Holy Spirit, who is called down upon each of the *confirmandi* every time the Church celebrates the Sacrament Confirmation, enliven your efforts and guide you as you selflessly prepare these teens to receive the gifts of the Holy Spirit.

Sincerely yours in Jesus, the Lord of Life,
Most Reverend Joseph F. Naumann
Archdiocese of Kansas City in Kansas

Reference Key

Compendium: Compendium of the Catechism of the Catholic Church, a summary of what Catholics believe.

CCC: Catechism of the Catholic Church

YouCat: Youth Catechism of the Catholic Church

1. Why did God create us?

In His loving goodness, God created us to know, love, and serve Him in this life and to be happy with Him for all eternity.

References:

> **Scripture:** John 17:3
>
> **Compendium:** 1
>
> **CCC:** 1–3
>
> **YouCat:** 1–2

2. How do we know that God exists?

We can know that God exists by honestly examining the world around us. God has also revealed Himself throughout human history, culminating in His sending us His Son Jesus, so that we may have a relationship with Him.

References:

> **Scripture:** Romans 1:20; Hebrews 1:1–4
>
> **Compendium:** 3–4, 9
>
> **CCC:** 36–38, 73
>
> **YouCat:** 4–7

3. How does God reveal Himself in the Old Testament?

God reveals Himself in the Old Testament as the Creator of the world. God's plan of loving goodness is gradually revealed through salvation history, as He remains steadfastly faithful to mankind despite the people's infidelity and sin.

References:

> **Scripture:** Genesis 1:1, 3:15; Isaiah 49:5–6; Hebrews 1:1
>
> **Compendium:** 6–8
>
> **CCC:** 68–72
>
> **YouCat:** 8
>
> **Vatican II:** *Dei Verbum (Dogmatic Constitution on Divine Revelation)*, 15: "The principal purpose to which the plan of the old covenant was directed was to prepare for the coming of Christ."

4. Who was Abraham?

Abraham was a Hebrew patriarch. Because of Abraham's great faith, God promised to bless all people through his descendants. God's promise to him was fulfilled in Christ, so Christians consider Abraham our father in faith.

References:

> **Scripture:** Genesis 12:1–3; Romans 4:1–21
>
> **Compendium:** 8, 26, 536
>
> **CCC:** 59–60, 145–46, 2570–73
>
> **YouCat:** 8, 471

5. Who was Moses?

Moses was the man God chose to lead the Israelites out of Egypt. God revealed His name to Moses, and also gave him the Ten Commandments on Mount Sinai.

References:
>**Scripture:** Exodus 3:1–12
>
>**Compendium:** 8, 537
>
>**CCC:** 62, 204–09, 2574–77
>
>**YouCat:** 472

6. Who was David?

David was the second King of Israel and the father of King Solomon, who built the temple in Jerusalem. Jesus, the promised Messiah and the King of the new and everlasting Israel, was born of King David's line.

References:
>**Scripture:** 1 Samuel 16:1–13; Matthew 1:1; Acts 13:21–22
>
>**Compendium**: 8, 538
>
>**CCC:** 709; 2578–80
>
>**YouCat:** 473

7. Is everything in the Bible true?

Scripture is *inspired*, meaning that God guided the human authors, who wrote only what God intended. Scripture is also *inerrant*, meaning that it teaches the truth, and not falsehood, taking into account the human author's intention and human limitations, as well as the literary genres of the time.

References:

> **Scripture:** 2 Timothy 3:16–17
>
> **Compendium:** 18–19
>
> **CCC:** 105–14
>
> **YouCat:** 14–16
>
> **Vatican II:** *Dei Verbum (Dogmatic Constitution on Divine Revelation),* 11: "The books of Scripture must be acknowledged as teaching solidly, faithfully and without error that truth which God wanted put into sacred writings for the sake of salvation."

8. Where do we turn to find out about the life of Jesus?

 We find out about the life of Jesus in the first four books of the New Testament: the Gospels of Matthew, Mark, Luke, and John. The Gospels provide inspired, eyewitness accounts of His life, teachings, death, and Resurrection.

References:

> **Scripture:** Luke 1:1–4
>
> **Compendium:** 22
>
> **CCC:** 124–27
>
> **YouCat:** 18

9. What is the Creed?

The Creed is a summary of the essential elements of the Christian faith. The most well-known creeds are the Apostles' Creed, which is often recited at the beginning of the Rosary, and the Nicene Creed, which is usually said at every Sunday Mass.

References:

    Scripture: 1 Corinthians 15:3–5

    Compendium: 33–35

    CCC: 185–97

    YouCat: 26

10. Why do we accept as true what the Church teaches in matters of faith and morals?

We accept Church teaching as true because the Church speaks with the authority of Christ Himself. Christ identifies with His Church and commissioned the Church to bring His teaching to all the world.

References:

    Scripture: Matthew 28:18–20; Luke 10:16;
    Acts 9:1–5; Ephesians 5:21–32; 1 Timothy 3:15

    Compendium: 16, 430

    CCC: 2032–37

    YouCat: 13, 24, 343–44

    Act of Faith: ". . . I believe these and all the truths which the Holy Catholic Church teaches because you [God] have revealed them, who can neither deceive nor be deceived."

11. Do Christians believe in one God or three Gods?

Christians believe in one God, who is a Trinity of Persons: Father, Son, and Holy Spirit.

References:

> **Scripture:** Matthew 28:19
>
> **Compendium:** 44, 48
>
> **CCC:** 249, 253–56
>
> **YouCat:** 35
>
> **Act of Faith:** "O my God, I firmly believe that you are one God in three divine Persons, Father, Son, and Holy Spirit."

12. Why does God, who is all-loving and all-powerful, allow suffering and evil?

God does not cause suffering and evil, but permits it as a possibility of human freedom. God allows evil in order to bring forth something good. In fact, from the greatest of all moral evils—the murder of His Son—He brought forth the greatest of all goods: the glorification of Christ and our redemption.

References:

> **Scripture:** Romans 8:28
>
> **Compendium:** 57–58
>
> **CCC:** 309–14
>
> **YouCat:** 51
>
> **St. Thomas Aquinas:** "For almighty God . . . , because He is supremely good, would never allow

any evil whatsoever to exist in His works if He were not so all-powerful and good as to cause good to emerge from evil itself."

13. What is our place in creation?

Man is the summit of creation, because God created us in His own image and entrusted us with the responsibility of caring for the world around us.

References:

Scripture: Genesis 1:26–28

Compendium: 63, 66–67

CCC: 343, 373, 2415–18

YouCat: 56–57

14. What is the soul?

The soul is the immortal, spiritual principle that gives life to the human body. The soul does not come from our parents but is created by God at conception. Our soul will be reunited with our resurrected body at the end of time.

References:

Scripture: Genesis 2:7; Matthew 10:28; 1 Corinthians 15:42–49

Compendium: 69–70

CCC: 362–68

YouCat: 62–63

Vatican II: *Gaudium et Spes (Pastoral Constitution on the Church in the Modern World)*, 14: "Man, though made of body and soul, is a unity. . . . Man may not despise his bodily life. Rather he is obliged to regard his body as good and to hold it in honor since God has created it and will raise it up on the last day."

15. What is original sin?

Original sin is the sin committed by Adam and Eve in choosing to disobey God. Because of original sin, everyone enters the world with a fallen nature and alienated from God. Jesus came as the "new Adam" to restore our friendship with God.

References:

Scripture: Genesis 3:1–13; Romans 5:12–14, 19
Compendium: 76–78
CCC: 388–89; 396–412
YouCat: 66–70

16. Who is Jesus?

Jesus is the eternal Son of God, the Second Person of the Blessed Trinity, who in the fullness of time became one like us in order to save us. The name "Jesus" means "God saves."

References:

Scripture: Matthew 1:21; Luke 1:31, 2:21; John 1:1, 14; Galatians 4:4–7; Hebrews 2:17, 5:15

Compendium: 81

CCC: 430–35

YouCat: 72–74

17. What does it mean to accept Jesus as Lord?

Whenever we call upon Jesus as "Lord," we acknowledge His divinity as the Son of God. We accept Him as Lord when we entrust our lives to Him and strive to live according to His teachings, which come to us through His Church.

References:

Scripture: Matthew 7:21; John 13:13, 20:28, 21:7; Romans 10:9; 1 Corinthians 12:3; Galatians 2:20; Philippians 2:5–11; Revelation 22:20–21

Compendium: 84

CCC: 446–51

YouCat: 75

Nicene Creed: "I believe in one Lord Jesus Christ, the Only Begotten Son of God, born of the Father before all ages."

18. Why did God become man?

God loves us so much that He sent His Son Jesus to reconcile us to Himself, to teach us how to live, and to share His own life with us.

References:

Scripture: John 3:16–17, 15:12; 1 John 4:9–10;
2 Peter 1:4

Compendium: 85

CCC: 456–60

YouCat: 76

Nicene Creed: "For us men and for our salvation He came down from heaven."

19. Why is Mary called the ever-virgin Mother of God and our Blessed Mother?

Mary was a virgin before, during, and after the birth of Jesus. She is the mother of Jesus, and Jesus is God. Therefore, she is truly the Mother of God. Mary is not only the mother of Jesus, the Son of God, but also the spiritual mother of all who believe in Him. All generations of Christians call her "blessed."

References:

Scripture: Matthew 1:23; Luke 1:26–38, 48;
John 2:1, 19:25–27; Revelation 12:17

Compendium: 95, 99–100

CCC: 495–501, 969, 971

YouCat: 80–82, 85

Council of Ephesus (AD 431): "If anyone does not profess that the Emmanuel is truly God and that the

Blessed Virgin is therefore the God-bearer . . . let him be anathema."

20. What happened at the Last Supper?

At the Last Supper, Jesus washed the feet of His Apostles, established the priesthood of the New Covenant, and instituted the Holy Eucharist during the course of a Passover meal as a memorial of His sacrifice.

References:

Scripture: Luke 22:19–20; John 13:1–15; 1 Corinthians 11:23–26

Compendium: 120

CCC: 610–11

YouCat: 99

21. Why did Jesus die on the Cross?

Christ freely accepted death on the Cross so as to bear the guilt of the whole world. In making Himself an offering for sin, He reconciled all people to God by His perfect love and obedience.

References:

Scripture: Matthew 20:28; John 12:32–33, 13:1; Galatians 2:20; Philippians 2:8

Compendium: 118–19, 122

CCC: 613–17

YouCat: 101

22. What is the Resurrection?

The Resurrection is the bodily rising of Jesus from the dead on the third day after His death on the Cross. Christ's victory over death is the crowning truth of our faith and the basis for our hope that we too will be raised with Christ.

References:

Scripture: Luke 24:1–7; John 11:25–26; 1 Corinthians 15:12–19

Compendium: 131

CCC: 651–58

YouCat: 104–08

23. Who is the Holy Spirit?

The Holy Spirit is the Third Person of the Blessed Trinity. The Holy Spirit is the personal love of the Father and the Son that is sent into our hearts at Baptism so that we might receive new life as children of God.

References:

Scripture: Matthew 28:19; John 14:16–17, 25–26; Acts 1:8; Romans 5:5, 8:14–17; Galatians 4:6

Compendium: 136, 138–39

CCC: 687–741

YouCat: 113–20

24. What happened on Pentecost?

Fifty days after His Resurrection, and just nine days after His Ascension into heaven, the Lord sent the Holy Spirit upon the disciples gathered in the Upper Room in prayer, thus beginning the age of the Church.

References:

Scripture: Acts 2:1–12

Compendium: 144

CCC: 731–32, 767

YouCat: 118

25. Why did Jesus establish the Church?

Jesus established the Church because God desires to save us not as isolated individuals, but as His family. The Church exists to extend the salvation won by Christ to everyone.

References:

Scripture: Matthew16:13–19; 28:19–20; Acts 10:35; Revelation 7:9–10

Compendium: 149–50, 152–53

CCC: 759, 763–66, 774–76, 781

YouCat:122–23

26. What are the four marks of the Church?

The marks of the Church are the four essential features of the Church and her mission. We believe that the Church is one, holy, catholic, and apostolic.

References:
Scripture: Matthew 28:18–20; John 17:20–21; Ephesians 2:19–21; 4:1–6; 5:25–27;
Compendium: 161, 165–66, 174
CCC: 811–12
YouCat: 129, 132–34, 137

27. What is the vocation of every Christian?

All baptized Christians are called by God to become like Jesus and, according to their state of life, to participate in the building up of the Church.

References:
Scripture: John 17:3; 1 Corinthians 9:16
Compendium: 188
CCC: 826–28, 897–900
YouCat: 138–39

28. Who is the Pope?

The Pope is the successor of St. Peter, the head of the Apostles to whom Christ entrusted the keys to the kingdom. He is the Bishop of Rome and the pastor of the entire Church as Christ's chosen representative on earth.

References:
Scripture: Isaiah 22:22; Matthew 16:13–19; Luke 22:31–32

Compendium: 182
CCC: 862, 880–82
YouCat: 141

29. What is religious life?

Religious life, also known as consecrated life, is a way of life approved by the Church in which one seeks to follow Christ as perfectly as possible. Consecrated life usually entails vows of poverty, chastity, and obedience after a period of formation and intensive prayer.

References:

Scripture: Matthew 19:21, 27–29; 1 Corinthians 7:32–35

Compendium: 192–93

CCC: 914–33, 944–45

YouCat: 145

30. How do Mary and the saints help us?

Mary and the saints give us examples of how to live out our Catholic faith, and they also pray for us.

References:

Scripture: 1 Corinthians 4:16, 11:1; Hebrews 12:1–2

Compendium: 195, 197
CCC: 954–57, 973–75
YouCat: 146–49

31. What is heaven?

Heaven is the state of perfect happiness for those who die in the grace of God and who have no need of further purification. We were created for eternal life with God in heaven.

References:

Scripture: 1 Corinthians 2:9, 13:12

Compendium: 209

CCC: 1023–29

YouCat: 158

32. What is purgatory?

Purgatory is the state of those who die in God's friendship, assured of their eternal salvation, but who still need purification to enter into the happiness of heaven. We can help the souls in purgatory by offering prayers and sacrifices for them.

References:
Scripture: 2 Maccabees 12:45–46; Matthew 12:32; 1 Corinthians 3:15; 1 Peter 1:7

Compendium: 210–11

CCC: 1030–32

YouCat: 159–60

33. Does hell exist?
The Church affirms the sad reality of eternal death, known as hell, for those who reject God's love. The main punishment of hell is separation from God, who alone can provide us the happiness for which we were created.

References:
Scripture: Matthew 10:28; 13:40–42; 25:41–46; Luke 16:19–31; 1 John 3:14–15

Compendium: 212–13

CCC: 1033–37

YouCat: 161–62

34. What happens to us at Baptism?
Baptism washes away original and personal sin, and it empowers us with divine grace to become children of

God. It is the door through which we enter the Church and begin a lasting relationship with Christ.

References:

Scripture: Acts 2:38; Romans 6:3–4; 2 Corinthians 5:17; 2 Peter 1:4

Compendium: 263

CCC: 1262–70

YouCat: 200

35. What is the Sacrament of Confirmation?

Confirmation is the sacrament in which we receive a special outpouring of the Holy Spirit like that of Pentecost to bear witness to Jesus and His Church. It strengthens and reinvigorates the gifts of the Holy Spirit received at Baptism.

References:

Scripture: Acts 8:14–17; 19:1–6

Compendium: 268

CCC: 1302–05, 1316

YouCat: 203–05

36. What is the Mass?

The celebration of the Eucharist, which includes both the liturgy of the Word and the liturgy of the Eucharist, is commonly called the "Mass." The Mass makes present in an unbloody manner Christ's once-for-all sacrifice on Calvary. It enables us to be transformed by Christ's victory over sin and death.

References:

Scripture: Malachi 1:11; Luke 22:7–20; 24:13–35;
Acts 2:42; Hebrews 7:25–27
Compendium: 275, 277, 280
CCC: 1332, 1341, 1345–47, 1362–68, 1382, 1408–10
YouCat: 212–14, 217, 221

37. What do Catholics believe concerning Christ's presence in the Eucharist?

The Eucharist is the Body and
Blood of Christ, really and
substantially present under the
appearance of bread and wine,
through which we are nourished in the faith and brought
into intimate communion with the Lord.

References:

Scripture: John 6:22–69; 1 Corinthians 11:23–30
Compendium: 282–86
CCC: 1373–81
YouCat: 208, 211

38. How should we prepare to receive Our Lord in Holy Communion?

We recall who it is we are receiving and approach the
sacrament with great reverence and awe, which should
be reflected in our demeanor and clothing. If we are in
a state of mortal sin, we should repent of our sin and

receive the Sacrament of Reconciliation before going to Communion.

The Church also requires us to fast for at least one hour from all foods and liquids, except for water and medicine, before receiving Holy Communion.

References:
Scripture: 1 Corinthians 11:27–29

Compendium: 291

CCC: 1384–87, 1415

YouCat: 220

39. Why do we need the Sacrament of Reconciliation?

Baptism gives us new life in Christ, but it does not free us from human weakness and the tendency to sin. The Sacrament of Reconciliation, or Confession, is Our Lord's way of allowing us to be reconciled with the Father after we sin.

References:
Scripture: John 20:19–23; 2 Corinthians 5:18–20

Compendium: 297–98

CCC: 1425–26, 1485–87

YouCat: 226

40. What does it mean to become a priest?

Through the Sacrament of Holy Orders, priests are ordained to act "in the person of Christ" by offering the sacrifice of the Mass, preaching the Gospel, and reconciling sinners to God, as co-workers of the bishop.

References:

Scripture: Luke 10:16; John 13:20, 20:19–23; Titus 1:5; James 5:14; Hebrews 7:15–17

Compendium: 328–29, 336

CCC: 1562–68, 1592

YouCat: 250, 254

41. What does the Church teach about marriage?

Marriage is an unbreakable covenant between one man and one woman that is ordered to the good of the spouses and the procreation and education of children. When it is between two Christians, marriage is a sacrament.

References:

Scripture: Genesis 2:21–24; Matthew 19:5–6; Ephesians 5:21–33

Compendium: 337–38, 341

CCC: 1601, 1603–05, 1659–1666

YouCat: 260–63

42. What is human freedom?

Freedom is the God-given power to be able to act of one's own accord. Because we are free, we are responsible for our actions. God expects us to use our freedom to choose what is good.

References:

Scripture: Genesis 2:15–17; John 8:31–32; Galatians 5:1

Compendium: 363–64

CCC: 1744–45

YouCat: 286–88

43. What is virtue?

A virtue is a good habit that helps us to do good and avoid evil.

References:

Scripture: Wisdom 8:7; 1 Corinthians 13:13; Philippians 4:8; Titus 2:11–13

Compendium: 377–79

CCC: 1803, 1833–44

YouCat: 299

44. What are sins?

Sins are deliberate thoughts, words, actions, or omissions that turn us away from God and His loving plan for us. Sins are harmful to us personally and they also injure our relationship with others.

References:

Scripture: Psalm 51; 1 Corinthians 6:9–11

Compendium: 392

CCC: 1849–51

YouCat: 315

St. Augustine: Sin is "an utterance, a deed, or a desire contrary to the eternal law."

Penitential Rite at Mass: "I confess to almighty God and to you, my brothers and sisters, that I have greatly sinned in my thoughts and in my words, in what I have done and in what I have failed to do . . ."

45. Are some sins more serious than others?

Mortal sin destroys God's life in us and, if we do not repent, could lead to damnation. For a sin to be mortal, it must be a serious matter and be committed with full knowledge and consent. *Venial* sins are less serious sins that nonetheless strain our relationship with God.

References:
> **Scripture:** 1 John 5:16–17
> **Compendium:** 394–96
> **CCC:** 1854–64
> **YouCat:** 316

46. What is the basis of human dignity?

The basis of human dignity is our creation in the image of God. All people share the same human nature and are called to share in the life of God. Every person is our "neighbor."

References:
> **Scripture:** Genesis 1:26–28; Luke 10:25–37
> **Compendium:** 2, 358, 412

CCC: 1700, 1704, 1929–33
YouCat: 280, 329–32

47. What is the purpose of the Commandments?

The Commandments are God's instruction manual for finding true and lasting happiness. They teach us how to love God with all our heart, and to love others as God loves us.

References:

Scripture: Exodus 20:1–17; Matthew 5:17–19; 19:16–19

Compendium: 434–35

CCC: 2052–63, 2080

YouCat: 348–51

48. What is so special about Sunday?

Sunday is the day of the week on which Jesus rose from the dead. Catholics set aside the Lord's Day for rest from their labors and above all for the celebration of the Eucharist. This fulfills the commandment to keep holy the Sabbath day.

References:

Scripture: Psalm 118:24; Matthew 28:1; Revelation 1:9–10

Compendium: 452–54

CCC: 2174–76, 2192–95

YouCat: 364–66

St. Justin Martyr (2nd century): "We all gather on the day of the sun, for it is the first day [after the Jewish Sabbath, but also the first day] when God, separating matter from darkness, made the world; and on this same day Jesus Christ our Savior rose from the dead."

49. What does it mean to be chaste?

Chastity is a moral virtue, related to temperance, which enables us to successfully integrate our sexuality into our personality. A chaste person lives his or her sexuality intentionally, motivated by love and not by selfish desires.

References:

Scripture: Sirach 26:15; Matthew 5:27–28; Galatians 5:22–23

Compendium: 488–91

CCC: 2337–50, 2394–96

YouCat:: 404–06

50. Why should we pray?

We pray because we were created with a longing for God. We pray to adore God and praise Him for His goodness, to seek His forgiveness for our sins, to thank Him for our blessings, and to seek His assistance.

References:

Scripture: Psalm 95:1–7; Luke 18:9–14; 1 Thessalonians 5:16–18; 1 Timothy 2:1–4,8; Revelation 7:11–12

Compendium: 534–35, 550

CCC: 2566–67, 2644

YouCat: 469–70, 483

St. Augustine: "You have made us for yourself, O Lord, and our heart is restless until it rests in you."

CPSIA information can be obtained
at www.ICGtesting.com
Printed in the USA
BVOW10s1600300516
449467BV00059B/114/P